ADVENT JOY

Advent Joy

Journeying towards the Nativity

Julien Chilcott-Monk

Gracewing

First published in England in 2015
by
Gracewing
2 Southern Avenue
Leominster
Herefordshire HR6 0QF
United Kingdom
www.gracewing.co.uk

ISBN 978 085244 875 5

Typeset by Gracewing

Cover design by Bernardita Peña Hurtado

CONTENTS

INTRODUCTION

T HIS ADVENT BOOK is a consideration of the Holy Incarnation in preparation for Christmas, encouraging the pilgrim to delve more deeply into the Christian Faith and to take note of the landmarks of our salvation history. The twenty-four stations take the pilgrim from the 1st December—no matter the date for Advent Sunday—to Christmas Eve. The book is a journey to Bethlehem and to Christmas through the writings that inspired the ancient Jews and that now inspire us as we read them in the light of the Resurrection of our Lord, and alongside the Nativity narratives of the gospels of Luke and Matthew. The cumulative effect and excitement of the journey from station to station will enlighten, it is to be hoped, and will prepare the pilgrim to embrace and celebrate anew the new-born infant at the first Mass of Christmas. The book offers a chance, layer by layer, to consider afresh the Holy Incarnation of our Lord and Saviour, from a time long before earth's clock was set in motion. The stations occasionally overlap and offer the chance to view an episode from a slightly different angle. While reading the meditation, the mind should be given free rein to explore further, and this will naturally turn into general prayer and intercession.

The daily meditation on the scriptural passage quoted takes the form of a personal and enquiring prayer to the Heavenly Father contained within the Paternoster. Each station concludes with appropriate and traditional Advent material from various sources.

Julien Chilcott-Monk
St Scholastica

Notes

The Scriptural quotations are taken from the Second Catholic Edition of the RSV revised according to *Liturgiam Authenticam*, 2001 and published by Ignatius Press, San Francisco 2006

The writer of Isaiah chapters 1–39 is referred to in the text as Isaiah; the writer of Isaiah chapters 40–55 as Isaiah II; the writer of Isaiah 56-66 as Isaiah III.

The Word

The First Station towards the Nativity

In the beginning was the Word, and the Word was with God, and the Word was God. He was in the beginning with God; all things were made through him, and without him was not anything made that was made. In him was life, and the life was the light of men. The light shines in the darkness, and the darkness has not overcome it.

John 1: 1–8

✠ In the Name of the Father, and of the Son, and of the Holy Spirit. Amen.

 ur Father, who art in heaven, hallowed be thy name. Thy kingdom come; thy will be done on earth, as it is in heaven.

Heavenly Father, you inspired John to leave us in no doubt that our Lord Jesus Christ, your Son, was ever with you, in the unity and love of the Holy Spirit. Our Lord, the Word, was ever your Divine Intention, was always there from the very beginning, to be begotten, to take flesh into your creation long before that radiation fireball you caused by thought, word or deed, that 'Big Bang' of unimaginable heat, which cooled and expanded to form the matter that would eventually produce countless galaxies and myriad stars and this ever-expanding universe, billions of years and many ages ago. You did not even then leave matters to their own devices because they had none without you. But further preparation was required before your plan could be put in place, because neither this planet Earth (even now only four and a half thousand million years old) nor indeed our Solar System, which contains it, had yet materialized at your command.

You invite us through this prologue to John's gospel, to consider further your creation and the Word made flesh and born into the world you created. It took your Holy Church many centuries to begin to understand something of your Triune Majesty even though you had already revealed through the ages much that was essential to our understanding—through prophets, and others you had chosen, through circumstances and situations and history itself. Before all worlds you knew your creation. The Word would illuminate it with life and ever be the guiding light of mankind into which the Word himself would enter at a point in that history. The Word would become true man and remain true God forever bound to you in an indissoluble bond.

Help me this Advent to grasp a little of your glorious and extraordinary plan, and of your Holy Incarnation, your gift of Christmas.

Give us this day our daily bread. And forgive us our trespasses, as we forgive those who trespass against us. And lead us not into temptation, but deliver us from evil. Amen.

Before the all-creating Lord
Let us rejoice with one accord,
Who made the worlds, the beaming sky,
The stars that glitter variously;
The sun, creation's central light,
The moon which softly decks the night,
All other orbs that gleam around,
Sea, land, hills, plains, and deeps profound.
Only Father, God alone;
Now and unto endless ages,
Thee their praise doth glorify,
Who for us and our salvation
Didst thine only Son send down.

From the Sarum sequence for the Fourth Sunday in Advent

Hail Mary, full of grace, the Lord is with thee; blessed art thou among women, and blessed is the fruit of thy womb, Jesus. Holy Mary, Mother of God, pray for us sinners, now and at the hour of our death. Amen

Glory be to the Father, and to the Son, and to the Holy
Spirit. As it was in the beginning, is now, and ever shall
be, world without end. Amen.

The Creation Narratives

The Second Station towards the Nativity

Then God said, 'Let us make man in our image, after our likeness…' So God created man in his own image, in the image of God he created him…

Genesis 1: 26a, 27a

In the day that the Lord God made the earth and the heavens, when no plant of the field was yet in the earth…then the Lord God formed man of dust from the ground…

Genesis 2: 4b, 5a, 7a

✠ In the Name of the Father, and of the Son, and of the Holy Spirit. Amen.

 UR FATHER, WHO art in heaven, hallowed be thy name. Thy kingdom come; thy will be done on earth, as it is in heaven.

Heavenly Father, is it not so that the origins of these creation stories date from a time of the great Mesopotamian empires when Canaan or Palestine was nothing more than a land of many tongues, many nationalities and displaced persons? Did these stories enter the oral traditions of the land long before the ancient Hebrews, your chosen people, entered the land and absorbed them as good teaching aids?

These stories help me to appreciate the vastness of the world you have created. You were patient in making a land ready for your chosen people through whom you would be revealed, but, nevertheless, you gave those earlier civilizations truths to understand and hold on to. At this time your innumerable attributes were seen as many 'gods' often in dispute with one another and with mankind. Out of these beginnings came your people with an understanding of you as the one true God, the only God.

In the first of the narratives, you have prepared everything for man; everything is in place for his creation. And this is not in the least out of keeping with your method and principal tool, that of evolution itself. Then you make us in your 'own image'. And we wrestle with this concept in one way or another. Might it be that your very Son gives you this image in which to create man? You know the future of the Word and the sight of the Word made flesh long before you embark upon any such work. And, in turn, does our Lord Jesus not give his face to your Triune Majesty? Does not Philip articulate the question on behalf of us all, on behalf of me—'Lord, show us the Father...' (John 14: 8) and elicit the reply 'He who has seen me has seen the Father...' (John 14: 9b)?

In the second of the narratives you show us how important we are to you, how important I am, and how much you love us. You create our world for us to do with as we please except that we must not let pride in ourselves influence how we behave to each other and to you. And, of course, that is just what we do; we put ourselves in place of you and we become our own idols. We serve self and little else and shut our ears to your call.

Help me, Almighty God, to hear and understand the teaching you gave to our forefathers.

Give us this day our daily bread. And forgive us our trespasses, as we forgive those who trespass against us. And lead us not into temptation, but deliver us from evil. Amen.

Let the choir devoutly bring
Welcome to th'eternal King,
And with one consent renew
The Creator's homage due.
Him angelic legions praise,
On his face enraptured gaze.
On him wait all earthly things
Till his nod their trial brings.
Awful he in judgements deep
Yet in might doth mercy keep.
Let thy saving health appear
Scattering perils far and near.
Bid the universe be clean,
Let us live in peace serene,
Till unto those realms we soar
Where thou reignest evermore.

From the Sarum sequence for the Second Sunday in Advent

Hail Mary, full of grace, the Lord is with thee; blessed art thou among women, and blessed is the fruit of thy womb, Jesus. Holy Mary, Mother of God, pray for us sinners, now and at the hour of our death. Amen

Glory be to the Father, and to the Son, and to the Holy Spirit. As it was in the beginning, is now, and ever shall be, world without end. Amen.

THE FALL:
ADAM AND EVE'S PRIDE

The Third Station towards the Nativity

'Have you eaten of the tree of which I commanded you not to eat?' The man said, 'The woman whom you gave to be with me, she gave me fruit of the tree, and I ate.'

Genesis 3: 11b, 12

✠ In the Name of the Father, and of the Son, and of the Holy Spirit. Amen.

 UR FATHER, WHO art in heaven, hallowed be thy name. Thy kingdom come; thy will be done on earth, as it is in heaven.

Is it so, perhaps, that when your creature—already in your own image—begins to exploit your gifts and emerges from Africa, adventurous, seeking fresh experience and advancement, he pauses in the moment he becomes aware of a slight to his self-importance? Does he promptly accuse you, the one for whom he possesses a natural and innate affection and awe, and defiantly shake his fist at you and make you, from that moment, secondary to his desires and comfort?

Man thought he had wrested his freedom from you but you had already given it to him. He was, of course, free to choose the path he should take in life. You had given him soul, and he rebelled and chose self-interest. He was always too proud to say sorry and soon realized that he was more often than not the author of his own misfortune. Is this what you inspired those ancient Mesopotamians to depict around the campfires and in the city palaces? It was they who saw the folly of man's pride and how it was responsible for an inevitable cascade of consequences, some attractive, others less so, all most dangerous. Even those ancients saw that your love had never diminished but that man placed a barrier between himself and your affection. And so they told the stories of Adam and Eve and got to the heart of the matter. Even in those far-off days, the story-tellers knew that they were all infected with the congenital defect we now term Original Sin; they knew that they were scarred and blemished. They surmised that man's blunder had occurred long before the establishment of the civilization they enjoyed; when he was naked and first defiantly shook his fist at you. Then, these ancients were not sure how many you were as they conferred divinity upon every natural action that occurred by your creative hand.

And as your chosen people subsequently arose in the land of Canaan, they were the inheritors of this teaching and were able gradually to develop their response to you as the only true God, and absorb the idea of how Adam and Eve represented humanity generally and every man and woman. And did you not cause them slowly and surely to expect what might be called a second Adam to heal the hurts caused by the first?

Assist me, Heavenly Father, to appreciate how, during the many centuries of your preparation of mankind, our love and understanding evolved in order to receive you in the Holy Incarnation 2,000 years ago.

Give us this day our daily bread. And forgive us our trespasses, as we forgive those who trespass against us. And lead us not into temptation, but deliver us from evil. Amen.

Creator of the stars of night,
Thy people's everlasting light,
Jesu, Redeemer, save us all,
And hear thy servants when they call.

Thou, grieving at the ancient curse
Should doom to death a universe,
Hast found the medicine full of grace,
To save and heal a ruined race
                    Conditor alme siderum, Tr. J. M. Neale

Hail Mary, full of grace, the Lord is with thee; blessed
art thou among women, and blessed is the fruit of thy
womb, Jesus. Holy Mary, Mother of God, pray for us
sinners, now and at the hour of our death. Amen

Glory be to the Father, and to the Son, and to the Holy
Spirit. As it was in the beginning, is now, and ever shall
be, world without end. Amen.

THE PROMISES TO ABRAHAM AND TO JACOB

The Fourth Station towards the Nativity

...and God said to him, 'Behold, my covenant is with you, and you shall be the father of a multitude of Nations. No longer shall your name be Abram, but your name shall be Abraham, for I have made you the father of a multitude of nations...I will make nations of you, and kings shall come forth from you.'

Genesis 17: 4-6

And the angel of the Lord called to Abraham...and said: 'I will indeed bless you, and I will multiply your descendants as the stars of heaven and as the sand which is on the sea shore.'

Genesis 22: 15-17

And God said to him, 'Your name is Jacob; no longer shall your name be called Jacob, but Israel shall be your name...I am God Almighty; be fruitful and multiply; a nation and a company of nations shall come from you, and kings shall spring from you. The land which I gave to Abraham and Isaac I will give to you, and I will give the land to your descendants after you.'

Genesis 35: 9-12

✠ In the Name of the Father, and of the Son, and of the Holy Spirit. Amen.

 UR FATHER, WHO art in heaven, hallowed be thy name. Thy kingdom come; thy will be done on earth, as it is in heaven.

You drew your people out of that great soup of humanity in Canaan, where remnants of many conquered nations mingled with settled farmers and wandering herdsmen. Abraham, the Father of Nations—in particular, the Hebrews—caught sight of you but did not have the uninterrupted knowledge of you enjoyed by later generations, for he carried with him from Haran to Ur and into Canaan his Mesopotamian heritage. Many centuries later, did the writers of Genesis not see their debt to Abraham, one of those nomadic herdsmen; his response to your call, and the important place he held in the evolution of their theology? Abraham and the Hebrews were, it seems, uniquely susceptible to you: and you made a promise to Abraham, which you renewed to his grandson, Jacob, upon whom you placed the responsibility for the future nation, and named him Israel. The writers of Genesis perceived that the beginnings of their faith in you as the One, True God could be associated with these significant occasions in those far-off days. They saw that the children of Abraham and those of his forebears were clearly of one family of peoples and nations, inextricably mixed and related, and descended from an original family somewhere, which we know was probably within the African cradle of humanity.

It is likely that Abraham did not apprehend you as the one and only God but caught important glimpses of you in a great morass of distractions, when the times were right. Doubtless he believed that you shared the heavenly stage with strange and terrifying divinities. We know different; we know you to be the one and only God, the God who has redeemed us, but that does not mean you do not have to share our altars of worship with our beloved, personal idols and false gods—our desires, the weaknesses, and so on, to which we readily succumb. And from time to time we replace you and blot you out with our selfishness and pride.

Inspire the leaders of all nations to seek and find your wisdom and love, and help me, Heavenly Father to do my part.

Give us this day our daily bread. And forgive us our trespasses, as we forgive those who trespass against us. And lead us not into temptation, but deliver us from evil. Amen.

Before me there was no God formed, nor shall there be after me: for to me shall every knee be bowed, and to me shall every tongue confess.
Antiphon, first Vespers, for the Third Sunday in Advent

Hail Mary, full of grace, the Lord is with thee; blessed art thou among women, and blessed is the fruit of thy womb, Jesus. Holy Mary, Mother of God, pray for us sinners, now and at the hour of our death. Amen

Glory be to the Father, and to the Son, and to the Holy Spirit. As it was in the beginning, is now, and ever shall be, world without end. Amen.

An Astounding Truth

The Fifth Station towards the Nativity

'Your father Abraham rejoiced that he was to see my day; he saw it and was glad.' The Jews then said to him, 'You are not yet fifty years old, and have you seen Abraham?' Jesus said to them, 'Truly, truly, I say unto you, before Abraham was, I am'

John 8: 56-8

He came to his own home, and his own people received him not.
John 1: 11

✠ In the Name of the Father, and of the Son, and of the Holy Spirit. Amen.

 UR FATHER, WHO art in heaven, hallowed be thy name. Thy kingdom come; thy will be done on earth, as it is in heaven.

When you told that group of questioners 'Abraham rejoiced to see my day' they were taken aback, even outraged. They had already accused you of madness, and, even, Samaritanism, a low insult at the time. Did you say gently to them that one day they would understand? But their eyes and minds were closed.

Did you, in fact, permit Abraham momentarily to glimpse the fruition of your Divine Plan and foresee your Holy Incarnation when he encountered those three angels who, by their very presence, gave him a foretaste of your Triune Majesty? (Genesis 18: 2) Your questioners had their minds closed against you and so entirely for our benefit elicited from you those astonishing words: 'Before Abraham was, *I am.*' Did the Father of the Nations gather from his encounter with the three angels that your Word would be made flesh; that you would pay the ransom for Adam and Eve's sin, and so redeem all humanity? Of course, his thoughts would not have run so deep, but you doubtless gave him sufficient reason to rejoice and we are able to see all at once, the gradual emergence of your Divine Plan. We see this in the history of the Hebrews, the Israelites, and the Jews of the time when you walked as man. We see your presence in the burning bush when you respond to Moses' question 'What shall I say to the sons of Israel?' You identify yourself as the God of Abraham, Isaac and Jacob, but Moses pressed you further: 'What is your name?' He is anxious to pin you down to give him a definitive answer, because from now on the Children of Israel gradually grasp that all gods but you are false and exist only in gold, bronze, stone and wood and other works of man's hands. Your replies are both unequivocal and, yet, mysterious. 'I am who I am' you say, adding 'tell them *I am* has sent you.' Immediately you inform your questioners in the Temple 'Before Abraham was, *I am*' you allow us to see something of our salvation history more clearly.

With Moses you set free your people from slavery in Egypt as they begin to know you as the only God and we see their Messianic hopes develop, their expectations of a Saviour and a King. We see the consequences of your revelation as *I am* to those questioners in the Temple, and we see how your death and Resurrection as man, secures for us and all mankind the freedom from the slavery of that inherited sin. Those men offered you up as the atoning sacrifice. But were there perceptive men among them, upon whom dawned the realization that as *I am* is the God of Moses so *I am* is before Abraham as he is at the time he addresses those angry men in the Temple in Jerusalem?

Heavenly Father, drench me with your love and understanding.

Give us this day our daily bread. And forgive us our trespasses, as we forgive those who trespass against us. And lead us not into temptation, but deliver us from evil. Amen.

In the beginning, and before the ages, the Word was God: he that is born unto us, the world's salvation.
Antiphon, Vespers during Octave of the Circumcision

Hail Mary, full of grace, the Lord is with thee; blessed art thou among women, and blessed is the fruit of thy womb, Jesus. Holy Mary, Mother of God, pray for us sinners, now and at the hour of our death. Amen

Glory be to the Father, and to the Son, and to the Holy Spirit. As it was in the beginning, is now, and ever shall be, world without end. Amen.

The People who walked in Darkness

The Sixth Station towards the Nativity

'The people who walked in darkness have seen a great light; those who dwelt in a land of deep darkness on them has light shined.'

Isaiah 9: 2

✠ In the Name of the Father, and of the Son, and of the Holy Spirit. Amen.

UR FATHER, WHO art in heaven, hallowed be thy name. Thy kingdom come; thy will be done on earth, as it is in heaven.

Your prophet Isaiah was speaking during King Ahaz's reign over the southern kingdom of Judah and at a time when Assyria was making threats against the northern kingdom of Israel, and showing all the signs of hostility to your people. He was speaking to his fellow countrymen; but he also speaks to us and enables us to trace the development of the continuous thread of Messianic hope, the hope you gave your people from the very beginning, the hope that was realized in your Holy Incarnation and in the Nativity at Bethlehem, and envisaged before all worlds. Isaiah saw hope on the horizon and that 'there will be no gloom for her that was in anguish'. (Isaiah 9: 1a)

Do you not desire your prophet's words to speak through the centuries, from the 8th century before the Word was made flesh, to this very day? Mankind has yet a long way to walk and many cannot see your glorious light often because we who are your children, obscure it from them by obscuring you with our idols of pride and self. Is it not so that your light should be revealed to others by the way we conduct ourselves and live our lives? Is this not one of the vocations you have given us? Why do we fail you every day? For us the Word took flesh in Mary's womb and was born in Bethlehem, David's city. Indeed, your names are 'Wonderful Counsellor' and 'Prince of Peace' as they are both 'Mighty God' and 'Everlasting Father'. (Isaiah 9: 6b)

We perceive in the oracles of prophets and poets truths that underlie and accompany the words, and caress them with a profundity of thought fuller and deeper than the words themselves might first suggest.

Help us to fulfil the vocation you give us; to allow your light to shine through us.

Give us this day our daily bread. And forgive us our trespasses, as we forgive those who trespass against us. And lead us not into temptation, but deliver us from evil. Amen.

Thou who dost each earthly throne
Rule by thy right hand alone,
Raise up thy great power and shine,
Show thy flock thy face divine.
Saving gifts on him bestow
Whom the prophets did foreshow.
From thy kingdom here on high,
Jesu, to our land draw nigh.

> From the Sarum sequence for the Third Sunday in Advent

Hail Mary, full of grace, the Lord is with thee; blessed art thou among women, and blessed is the fruit of thy womb, Jesus. Holy Mary, Mother of God, pray for us sinners, now and at the hour of our death. Amen

Glory be to the Father, and to the Son, and to the Holy Spirit. As it was in the beginning, is now, and ever shall be, world without end. Amen.

THE COMING OF JOHN THE BAPTIST IS FORETOLD

The Seventh Station towards the Nativity

'Speak tenderly to Jerusalem, and cry to her that her warfare is ended, that her iniquity is pardoned…'

Isaiah 40: 2

✠ In the Name of the Father, and of the Son, and of the Holy Spirit. Amen.

 OUR FATHER, WHO art in heaven, hallowed be thy name. Thy kingdom come; thy will be done on earth, as it is in heaven.

For whom was Isaiah II yearning? How did he see that your mercy was falling so readily upon your people? The northern Kingdom of Israel had long been dispersed and much of the existing population imported from other lands; the southern Kingdom of Judah was now in exile in Babylon and it was obvious that pride and self-seeking had led them there, for you had given them, as you have given me, complete freedom of will. You inspired this prophet to show that you always care most earnestly for your people—a nation, a divided nation and then a disintegrated nation—as a father cares for a wayward child. I too am that wayward child. Once again, you would guide that wayward nation to her homeland as you had done so through Moses about one thousand years before. And the way would be made easy for their return this time because Cyrus and the Persian armies were in the wings and it would not be long before Cyrus would break the Babylonian empire and permit the exilic Judeans a safe return home. But this return to the homeland and restoration of the capital would be the beginning of a rather different life for this remnant of Israel, ending in Greek and Roman domination and, ultimately, near-annihilation. You chose this unlikely scenario for your Holy Incarnation and the birth of the Word made flesh, a scenario that was truly *down-to-earth*.

Isaiah II sets the scene and prepares the people for what is to come and we recognize in John the Baptist's ministry that same role. John is indeed required, as your prophet asserts, to 'prepare the way of the Lord, make straight in the desert a highway for our God...the even ground shall become level and the rough places a plain.' (Isaiah 40: 3, 4b) This time, however, the release from exile is the salvation of the whole of mankind. Your evangelist, Luke, cites this passage in his Gospel, and you yourself show us the purpose of your cousin's work when you refer to the prophet Malachi. 'Behold, I send my messenger to prepare the way before me...' (Matthew 11: 10; Malachi 3: 1a) Your prophet Malachi could see the dissatisfaction of the people even after they had returned to Jerusalem from Babylon; still they yearned for more, and in due time you would give the world that which was your Divine Intention from the beginning.

And so, the focus of your saving action would now be David's first city, the city of Bethlehem, within Judah, the southern remnant of Israel, and David's own tribe from which sprang both Joseph and Mary.

Let us, heavenly Father, understand better your mysterious ways in order that we may be equipped to fulfil the vocations you would have us fulfil.

Give us this day our daily bread. And forgive us our trespasses, as we forgive those who trespass against us. And lead us not into temptation, but deliver us from evil. Amen.

Drop down, ye heavens, from above, and let the skies pour down righteousness.
Comfort ye, comfort ye my people; my salvation shall not tarry: I have blotted out as a thick cloud thy transgressions: Fear not, for I will save thee: for I am the Lord thy God, the Holy One of Israel, thy Redeemer.

From the Advent Prose

Hail Mary, full of grace, the Lord is with thee; blessed art thou among women, and blessed is the fruit of thy womb, Jesus. Holy Mary, Mother of God, pray for us sinners, now and at the hour of our death. Amen

Glory be to the Father, and to the Son, and to the Holy Spirit. As it was in the beginning, is now, and ever shall be, world without end. Amen.

The Coming of John the Baptist

The Eighth Station towards the Nativity

He came for testimony, to bear witness to the light, that all might believe through him. He was not the light, but came to bear witness to the light.

John 1: 7, 8

✠ In the Name of the Father, and of the Son, and of the Holy Spirit. Amen.

 UR FATHER, WHO art in heaven, hallowed be thy name. Thy kingdom come; thy will be done on earth, as it is in heaven.

Was John the Baptist the eccentric and curious figure
we imagine, emerging from the desert? Was it of
significance that he arose out of the wilderness of
Judea? Maybe if we listen to his words carefully we
find him articulate and learned in the Scriptures and
clearly well-prepared for the task before him. Had he
been trained in the Scriptures by the community of the
Essenes who lived in the desert regions to the northwest of the Dead Sea? He arose out of the desert to
begin a ministry preaching repentance and baptizing
in the River Jordan. He arose, did he not, out of the
past, out of an era that had already passed by? He
arose out of the wilderness to point the way to Salvation just as Israel emerged from the wilderness on her
way from Egypt to the Promised Land. He arose from
the past to herald the new age, to herald something
already promised that would turn the world inside
out. Is John, then, not the bridge between the two
worlds, from the mists of the past to the clear light of
the present age?

People asked him to identify himself. 'I am not the
Christ.' 'Are you Elijah?' 'I am not.' They asked him:
'Are you the prophet [i.e. Moses]?' 'No.' They asked
him to explain himself and he then quoted the prophet
Isaiah revealing that he was the voice crying in the
wilderness 'Make straight the way of the Lord'. Your
worthy cousin's vocation was clear to him, that he was
called to shake the people out of their complacency,
prick their consciences and stir them to personal repentance. Soon you would pay the price of mankind's
Original sin and the graces given us in Baptism in the
name of the Father, Son and Holy Spirit would seal us
from the guilt of that sin and allow us to be one with
you. John pointed to you as the 'Lamb of God' (John 1:

29)—that is the one marked for sacrifice—and asserted that he was inspired to point to you by Divine authority. It was not his affection for you as cousin and his own powers of discernment that identified you to him.

Later, in order to underline the duty he has already fulfilled, he asks you from his prison cell, for final clarification and for his benefit, the benefit of others and for us. 'Are you he who is to come, or shall we look for another?' And your answer is unequivocal as you ask his messengers 'Go and tell John what you hear and see: the blind receive their sight and the lame walk, lepers are cleansed and the deaf hear, and the dead are raised up, and the poor have good news preached to them'. (John 11: 4, 5) You knew that your words would give confirmation and comfort to John because he would know well the words of Isaiah: 'In that day the deaf shall hear the words of a book, and out of their gloom and darkness the eyes of the blind shall see. The meek shall obtain fresh joy in the Lord, and the poor among man shall exult in the Holy One of Israel.' (Isaiah 29: 18, 19)

Let us not ignore those who point the way and guide us toward your will.

Give us this day our daily bread. And forgive us our trespasses, as we forgive those who trespass against us. And lead us not into temptation, but deliver us from evil. Amen.

Let thine example, holy John, remind us,
Ere we can meetly sing thy deeds of wonder,
Hearts must be chastened, and the bonds that bind us
Broken asunder!

Ut queant laxis, Tr R. Ellis Roberts

Hail Mary, full of grace, the Lord is with thee; blessed art thou among women, and blessed is the fruit of thy womb, Jesus. Holy Mary, Mother of God, pray for us sinners, now and at the hour of our death. Amen

Glory be to the Father, and to the Son, and to the Holy Spirit. As it was in the beginning, is now, and ever shall be, world without end. Amen.

The Peace that will come into the World

The Ninth Station towards the Nativity

Of the increase of his government and of peace there will be no end, upon the throne of David, and over his kingdom.

Isaiah 9: 7

✠ In the Name of the Father, and of the Son, and of the Holy Spirit. Amen.

 ur Father, who art in heaven, hallowed be thy name. Thy kingdom come; thy will be done on earth, as it is in heaven.

How do we understand your peace and how do we
define it? Is it not so much more than that which is
sought by a besieged city or a warring town? Your
evangelist, Luke, is certain that on the night of the birth
of the Word, the angels in heaven were unable to
contain their joy and keep silent, declaring peace
among men with whom you were pleased. (Luke 2:
14) Is the peace envisaged through the eye of Isaiah,
the same peace? For Isaiah it must have included not
only the cessation of conflict and battle, but also
something of general tranquillity. In describing you in
the richest terms he can muster, do you not inspire him
to tread close to the matter? 'Wonderful Counsellor'
and 'Mighty God' show his understanding of your vast
breadth and that both these attributes are those of a
father, an 'Everlasting Father' a father who is always
a father and eternally a father to his creatures. Then he
adds to his list 'Prince of Peace' as if to make 'Peace' a
place, natural and supernatural; perhaps an *actual* state
rather than a figurative one. Is, then, this place of
'Peace' an environment, a place in which to be? Do you
not guide us to this place through Isaiah's words and
when armed with these words we are equipped to
reflect upon Luke's certainty of the angels' cry? We
then begin to understand the peace that is given to
those with whom you are pleased, or simply to those
who will it. You love your creatures equally but do
those who seek you by whatever means you have
given them—their vocations and callings—find themselves in that place of peace? Is it, therefore, none other
than the kingdom where you reign as Christ the King?

Further, is this kingdom the passageway to Heavenly eternity in you? Is it sufficient that we seek you
and yearn for your goodness? Is this place a place we

can assume or attain if we strive to live our lives as though we were citizens of heaven; if we strive for the standards and values of heaven rather than those by which we are inclined to live on earth? It is surely there that true peace is found because this kingdom is to have part with you, within this passageway to Heaven.

May we all understand the implications of living our earthly lives, as though citizens of heaven.

Give us this day our daily bread. And forgive us our trespasses, as we forgive those who trespass against us. And lead us not into temptation, but deliver us from evil. Amen.

The kingdom of heaven is likened unto a net, cast into the sea, which gathered of every kind: which, when it was filled, they drew to the land...

From the Antiphon for first Vespers of a Virgin

Hail Mary, full of grace, the Lord is with thee; blessed art thou among women, and blessed is the fruit of thy womb, Jesus. Holy Mary, Mother of God, pray for us sinners, now and at the hour of our death. Amen

Glory be to the Father, and to the Son, and to the Holy Spirit. As it was in the beginning, is now, and ever shall be, world without end. Amen.

The Suffering Servant

The Tenth Station towards the Nativity

'It is too light a thing that you should be my servant…I will give you as a light to the nations, that my salvation may reach to the end of the earth.'

Isaiah 49: 6b

'Behold, my servant shall prosper, he shall be exalted…As many were astonished at him; his appearance was so marred. He was despised and rejected by men…Surely he has borne our griefs and carried our sorrows; yet we esteemed him stricken, struck down by God…'

Isaiah 52: 13; 53: 3a, 4

✠ In the Name of the Father, and of the Son, and of the Holy Spirit. Amen.

 UR FATHER, WHO art in heaven, hallowed be thy name. Thy kingdom come; thy will be done on earth, as it is in heaven.

A Messiah who is also the Suffering Servant is shown
to us in the prose and poetry of Isaiah II and in those
of the post-exilic Isaiah III. Through these writings you
give us an indication of the human nature of the
Messiah. That he must suffer is the consequence of the
history of mankind as represented by your chosen
people. The Suffering Servant Messiah is necessary for
the redemption of the world. And do you not point out
many times the need of a Christ who has to suffer?
Indeed, you admonish Peter as 'Satan' when he seems
to obstruct what is the Divine Intention. (Matthew 4: 10)
This is our lesson too: if the Messiah does not suffer he
cannot be sacrificed and the ransom cannot be paid.
Man, in order to be redeemed, must offer up the
Messiah as a willing sacrifice to God. It is a hard truth
to grasp but just as the innocent lamb is taken from the
hillside in Bethlehem to fulfil the requirements of
Temple worship, so too must the perfect man, innocent
of wrong, be the only acceptable offering. And you
lovingly and generously poured yourself into humanity for the purpose.

   From their exile in Babylon, your people had time
to reflect, and Isaiah II shows how, as Creator, you
gave life to the people on earth and subsequently made
a special arrangement with your chosen people. Your
people, however, rejected all that was lavished upon
them and drew away from you. Isaiah II tells the
people about a Divine servant who will have to endure
suffering before he is 'raised up'. Your promise to
restore Israel is a promise to the world, for Israel now
represents the whole of humanity.

   Do you not permit the prophet to allude to the
sufferings of the Word made flesh? Peter, at first, failed
to understand but his failure allows us to learn the

lesson by your very words. Any obstruction to the Divine will is the placing of ourselves and our pride in the way of that will. Satan is born of such obstruction and inhibition to the Word of God. If we are instrumental in this, we give flesh to Satan and allow ourselves to represent him.

Christ has already driven away the consequences of the sin of Adam and Eve and all sin by his once-and–for-all sacrifice and has bought our redemption. Let us never fail to thank you for all your beneficence.

Give us this day our daily bread. And forgive us our trespasses, as we forgive those who trespass against us. And lead us not into temptation, but deliver us from evil. Amen.

O Saviour of the world, who by thy Cross and precious Blood hast redeemed us; save us and help us, we humbly beseech thee.

Antiphon *Salvator Mundi* for Good Friday

Hail Mary, full of grace, the Lord is with thee; blessed art thou among women, and blessed is the fruit of thy womb, Jesus. Holy Mary, Mother of God, pray for us sinners, now and at the hour of our death. Amen

Glory be to the Father, and to the Son, and to the Holy Spirit. As it was in the beginning, is now, and ever shall be, world without end. Amen.

The Glory of God

The Eleventh Station towards the Nativity

'Arise, shine; for your light has come, and the glory of the Lord has risen upon you.'

Isaiah 60: 1

The true light that enlightens every man was coming into the world.

John 1: 9

✠ In the Name of the Father, and of the Son, and of the Holy Spirit. Amen.

 ur Father, who art in heaven, hallowed be thy name. Thy kingdom come; thy will be done on earth, as it is in heaven.

Now it is Isaiah III who speaks so eloquently of your light and glory, the brightness of your omnipotence — the light that began your creative design (Genesis 1: 3) and the light of John 1: 7, both emanating from the same source. Your prophet here speaks from the point of view of the returned exile from Babylon. The city of Jerusalem would again flourish and be re-established in glory and we can read these words by the light of your Holy Incarnation and Nativity. Indeed, you gave Isaiah III understanding of the depth of that light because upon that light he built up hope and expectation among the remnant of Israel returning to their homeland, in particular to their capital, Jerusalem, of the southern Kingdom of Judah. Yes, they could be reminded of your bounty and mercy, for you had saved them twice — from slavery and from exile.

It was under your glory and your light so needed by those who walked in darkness and spoken of by the first Isaiah. (Isaiah 9) This is the light by which all nations should walk (Isaiah 60: 3) and is the light that Simeon held in his arms declaring it to be the light that would lighten the lives of the Gentiles, of all mankind. (Luke 2: 28 — 32)

To Jerusalem men and women would flock once again and it would become a successful centre of commerce as it once was. Gentiles would trade as before: 'A multitude of camels shall cover you…all those from Sheba shall come. They shall bring gold and incense.' (Isaiah 60: 6) And we know how those merchants would visit Jerusalem a few hundred years into the future along with some wise men from Babylon, that very place of exile. They would follow the light of a particularly bright star you had placed in the firmament, which star would reflect the glory and light of the Holy Infant lying in a manger of straw. These first Gentiles to be enlightened would return to their own country without their gold, frankincense and myrrh but carrying with them your light, which they could not suppress or hide.

We pray that we may ever reflect the light that enlightens all men.

Give us this day our daily bread. And forgive us our trespasses, as we forgive those who trespass against us. And lead us not into temptation, but deliver us from evil. Amen.

The kings of Tharsis and of the isles shall give presents: the kings of Arabia and Saba shall bring gifts: all kings of the earth shall fall down before him: and all nations shall do him service.

Offertory for Epiphany of our Lord

Hail Mary, full of grace, the Lord is with thee; blessed art thou among women, and blessed is the fruit of thy womb, Jesus. Holy Mary, Mother of God, pray for us sinners, now and at the hour of our death. Amen

Glory be to the Father, and to the Son, and to the Holy Spirit. As it was in the beginning, is now, and ever shall be, world without end. Amen.

WISDOM IS WITH GOD FROM THE VERY BEGINNING

The Twelfth Station towards the Nativity

'With you is Wisdom who knows your works and was present when you made the world, and who understands what is pleasing in your sight and what is right according to your commandments. Send her forth from the holy heavens, and from the throne of your glory send her...'

The Wisdom of Solomon 9: 9, 10a

'I, Wisdom, dwell in prudence...I love those who love me, and those who seek me diligently find me. Ages ago I was set up, at the first, before the beginning of the earth. When there were no depths I was brought forth... When he established the heavens, I was there...'

Proverbs 8: 12, 17, 23, 24, 27

'And thus the paths of those on earth were set right, and men were taught what pleases you, and were saved by Wisdom.'

The Wisdom of Solomon 9: 18

*In the beginning was the Word, and the Word was with God,
and the Word was God. He was in the beginning with God;
all things were made through him, and without him was not
made anything that was made.*

John 1: 1–3

✠ In the Name of the Father, and of the Son, and of the
Holy Spirit. Amen.

 UR FATHER, WHO art in heaven, hallowed be thy
name. Thy kingdom come; thy will be done on
earth, as it is in heaven.

The ancients saw the breadth and depth and height of
your Divine action in the world and in the heavens as
Wisdom and, further, began gradually to see your
Wisdom as, perhaps, an idea, a concept, even your
Divine Plan or Intention. Were they far from the Truth?
But you, surely, had guided them to these conclusions.
Was it not in your Wisdom that the Word was with
you in the beginning? The writer of Proverbs is nearly
there in the declaration that Wisdom was in the
beginning before you began your work. (Proverbs 8:
22) and then, John, having himself seen the Word made
flesh, allows us a glimpse at the mystery of your Triune
Majesty in the prologue to his Gospel. Is it not the
Word, your Son, from whom you gave man face, who
gave us your face to gaze upon? Is this not the eternal
Truth and mystery of your oneness with the Son bound
within a Unity of love in the Holy Spirit? Have you
not inspired us towards this destination? The writer
of Wisdom comes close to the point with the words:
'Who has learned your counsel unless you have given

Wisdom and sent your Holy Spirit from on high?'
(Wisdom of Solomon 9: 17) And Paul gets to the heart
of the matter with 'Christ [the Word] is the Power and
Wisdom of God.' (1 Corinthians 1: 24b) and joins the
two ideas once and for all.

Your Wisdom is your Word is our Lord.

Give us this day our daily bread. And forgive us our
trespasses, as we forgive those who trespass against
us. And lead us not into temptation, but deliver us
from evil. Amen.

*O Wisdom, which camest out of the mouth of the Most High,
and richest from one end to another, most mightily, and
beautifully ordering all things: come and teach us the way
of prudence.*

First Great 'O' Antiphon

Hail Mary, full of grace, the Lord is with thee; blessed
art thou among women, and blessed is the fruit of thy
womb, Jesus. Holy Mary, Mother of God, pray for us
sinners, now and at the hour of our death. Amen

Glory be to the Father, and to the Son, and to the Holy
Spirit. As it was in the beginning, is now, and ever shall
be, world without end. Amen.

THE IMMACULATE CONCEPTION

The Thirteenth Station towards the Nativity

*And behold an angel of the Lord stood before her saying:
'Fear not, Mary, for thou hast found grace before the Lord
of all things, and thou shalt conceive of his Word.'*

Protevangelium

*And he came to her and said, 'Hail, full of grace, the Lord is
with you!'…And the angel said to her, 'Do not be afraid,
Mary, for you have found favour with God. And behold you
will conceive in your womb and bear a son, and you shall call
his name Jesus…and be called the Son of the Most High…'*

Luke 1: 28-32

✠ In the Name of the Father, and of the Son, and of the Holy Spirit. Amen.

 UR FATHER, WHO art in heaven, hallowed be thy name. Thy kingdom come; thy will be done on earth, as it is in heaven.

Your preparations were meticulous; the Mother of the Word would have all the advantages of your saving power. To this girl in her simplicity, drawn from a tribe of your chosen people, you gave the privileges that came to us by your Passion, Death and Resurrection, and in our Baptism, when we were made one with you. Did you not choose Mary to bridge your natural and supernatural worlds? Did your angel not announce to her that she would conceive through the Holy Spirit, house, and give birth to the Word made flesh? You gave her the freedom to refuse this daunting task because you needed her positive and unswerving response.

How was our Lady Mary set aside? Was Mary not the natural child of Joachim and Ann, one of a number, maybe, Salome among them? And yet we believe you set her aside in a particular way—in a way no one could possibly see; you sanctified her and saved her from the stain of Original and inherited sin, and lavished upon her the grace provided in Baptism from the moment of her conception. Was it not the only way in which a worthy creature could be found and prepared for so great a vocation? Your revelations are delivered to your prophets, guides and theologians in their contemplation. Did not Luke himself gather from Mary the words of your messenger? It is likely. Indeed was his record not much-cited, copied down and repeated throughout early Christendom? Though simple enough, were not the angel's words of penetrating significance? 'Hail, full of grace, the Lord is with you!' and '...you have found favour with God.' So is it not clear and certain that the sin of Adam and Eve sent coursing through our DNA giving us a predilection for pride and the consequences of it, was never present in Mary? How could it have been otherwise?

May we ever honour Mary, your Mother who prays for us now and at the hour of our death.

Give us this day our daily bread. And forgive us our trespasses, as we forgive those who trespass against us. And lead us not into temptation, but deliver us from evil. Amen.

The God whom earth, and sea, and sky,
Adore, and laud, and magnify,
Who o'er their threefold fabric reigns,
The Virgin's spotless womb contains.
Quem terra, pontus, aethera, Tr. J M Neale

Hail Mary, full of grace, the Lord is with thee; blessed art thou among women, and blessed is the fruit of thy womb, Jesus. Holy Mary, Mother of God, pray for us sinners, now and at the hour of our death. Amen

Glory be to the Father, and to the Son, and to the Holy Spirit. As it was in the beginning, is now, and ever shall be, world without end. Amen.

A Virgin shall conceive and bear a Son

The Fourteenth Station towards the Nativity

'Therefore the Lord himself will give you a sign. Behold, a virgin shall conceive and bear a son, and shall call his name Immanuel.'

Isaiah 7: 14

✠ In the Name of the Father, and of the Son, and of the Holy Spirit. Amen.

 UR FATHER, WHO art in heaven, hallowed be thy name. Thy kingdom come; thy will be done on earth, as it is in heaven.

In the midst of Isaiah's prophesies, his oracles, and in his counsel of King Ahaz, you planted this kernel— that the House of David would again be of the utmost significance for your chosen people, not, however, in any way that they might envisage. This would be the climax of your Divine Plan sitting upon the elaborate history of your people through which ran the path to this destination. For this you made yourself known in glimpses to the Patriarchs of old; for this you revealed yourself as the one true God to Moses and to those you called out of slavery in Egypt; for this you patiently and mercifully forgave your people as they constantly disobeyed and rejected you for false gods; for this you suffered the division of your people, their dispersal by the Assyrians and exile by the Babylonians. But sown here in Isaiah's words is the seed of comfort for the future, your promise to your people. At this time the destruction of Jerusalem and the enforced trek to Babylon were in the future, so worse was yet to be endured. You planted this and it gave wider and deeper meaning for the successors of those who first heard it. And those who came centuries later saw you with us, God with us, the Word made flesh; and you have remained with us in the Holy Sacrament of the Altar ever since, and we have become one with you in Holy Baptism.

Isaiah, as we do, saw pride as the principal sin and the cause of all consequential sin: it was to eradicate our guilt and to pay the penalty for Adam's sin and mine that you came to us, that you were born of a virgin, and that you fulfilled your ministry and mission.

Forgive our proud ways and what they cause us to do.

Give us this day our daily bread. And forgive us our trespasses, as we forgive those who trespass against us. And lead us not into temptation, but deliver us from evil. Amen.

O Virgin of virgins, how shall this be? For neither before thee was any like thee, nor shall there be after. Daughters of Jerusalem, why marvel ye at me? The thing which ye behold is a divine mystery.
The Eighth Great 'O' Antiphon (Sarum)

Hail Mary, full of grace, the Lord is with thee; blessed art thou among women, and blessed is the fruit of thy womb, Jesus. Holy Mary, Mother of God, pray for us sinners, now and at the hour of our death. Amen

Glory be to the Father, and to the Son, and to the Holy Spirit. As it was in the beginning, is now, and ever shall be, world without end. Amen.

The Annunciation

The Fifteenth Station towards the Nativity

'And behold, you will conceive in your womb and bear a son, and you shall call his name Jesus... The Holy Spirit will come upon you, and the power of the Most High will overshadow you; therefore the child to be born will be called holy, the Son of God.'

Luke 1: 31, 35

✠ In the Name of the Father, and of the Son, and of the Holy Spirit. Amen.

 ur Father, who art in heaven, hallowed be thy name. Thy kingdom come; thy will be done on earth, as it is in heaven.

We believe that your messenger's words were given to Luke by our Lady herself and we understand by those words of greeting that you preserved her from the inheritance of Adam and Eve, the inheritance from which you released us all by your once-and-for-all sacrifice and by our sharing that sacrifice with you in Baptism. She was an eligible creature, eligible to receive the detail of the assignment you were proposing. But did you not require something from Mary? You did not make a demand of her without expecting or desiring a response. Indeed, your Blessed Mother's response was most necessary.

Mary expressed fear and astonishment at the messenger's greeting but there was much more to come as he revealed the task and the significance of the role she would play. 'How can this be, since I have no husband?' she pointed out. The angel told her that your Holy Spirit would *overshadow* her, as your Holy Spirit overshadowed the waters of this earth in the very beginning of your creative impulse. But the proposition would have sounded hardly any less daunting to Mary for that explanation. I grumble at much you ask of me, although you ask from us, I believe, only as much as is within our capabilities and scope. Mary had yet to respond: she knew that absolute trust and faith in you would be required, which, from time to time, would be tested, as you test us all. Indeed, soon enough, she would hear Simeon's terrible prediction of the seven swords, the sorrows, which would pierce her heart.

Nevertheless, with this sudden calling of such exquisite privilege tinged, probably, with daunting terror ringing in Mary's ears, she responds to you and give us the example of selfless acquiescence—the antidote to the first Eve's connivance with Satan, the obstructer—

with the words 'Behold I am the handmaid of the Lord; let it be to me according to your word.' And, of course, your word was the Word. Her selfless acceptance of your will was her generous and humble response; her co-operation in this most holy enterprise.

Teach me, Heavenly Father, to listen to your will.

Give us this day our daily bread. And forgive us our trespasses, as we forgive those who trespass against us. And lead us not into temptation, but deliver us from evil. Amen.

Hail, O Star that pointest
Towards the port of heaven,
Thou to whom as maiden
God for Son was given.

When the salutation
Gabriel has spoken,
Peace was shed upon us,
Eva's bonds were broken.
Ave maris Stella, Tr. A. Rawnsley

Hail Mary, full of grace, the Lord is with thee; blessed art thou among women, and blessed is the fruit of thy womb, Jesus. Holy Mary, Mother of God, pray for us sinners, now and at the hour of our death. Amen

Glory be to the Father, and to the Son, and to the Holy Spirit. As it was in the beginning, is now, and ever shall be, world without end. Amen.

The Visitation

The Sixteenth Station towards the Nativity

In those days Mary arose and went with haste to the hill country, to a city of Judah, and she entered the house of Zechariah and greeted Elizabeth.

(Luke 1: 39)

✠ In the Name of the Father, and of the Son, and of the Holy Spirit. Amen.

 ur Father, who art in heaven, hallowed be thy name. Thy kingdom come; thy will be done on earth, as it is in heaven.

Your evangelist, anxious to record for the benefit of succeeding generations, pieced together these early episodes in your life as man. 'A city of Judah' seems vague but was it not situated somewhere to the northwest of the Dead Sea? Mary's child was not thought to be in peril even though the journey she took would have been not without some discomfort. You were to experience the whole of the human condition in all its triumphs, and terrors; its joys and sorrow; its wit and its woe.

Allow me to envisage this meeting of the mothers-to-be. The house, a stone affair, larger than some, though not grand in any way, would have been what Mary found. This would become the household of the last of the 'Old Testament-style' prophets—he who would bring an end to an era that began with Moses, and prepare the world for the salvation they longed for.

Why did you move Mary to visit Elizabeth? Was it the special bond she had with the older woman only recently revealed by your messenger? Was it that she wished to embrace Elizabeth as a fellow traveller on the road to the final stages of salvation history? John would be the signpost along that road. Mary knew but little of what was in store and, indeed, her cousin would have been unaware that her son would be lost to Herod the Tetrarch and slain in a dungeon. Here, however, they greet each other in full assurance of hope for humanity and the boy who will be called 'the Baptist' leaps and kicks in the womb. Coming so close to your presence did you not, at this stage, sanctify John?

During her stay, how did Mary communicate with Zechariah? He was to remain dumb until the birth of John because you admonished him for his scepticism. Thus the older generation were silenced for a season in Zechariah, to reflect upon their habitual rejection of the prophets through the ages, and their deafness to your call.

Mary was so moved with joy at her cousin's greeting: '...And blessed is she who believed that there would be a fulfilment of what was spoken to her from the Lord' that all the thrills of her absolute faith in you and love for you expressed themselves in a spontaneous song of praise.

May we never be afraid to share the joy of our salvation.

Give us this day our daily bread. And forgive us our trespasses, as we forgive those who trespass against us. And lead us not into temptation, but deliver us from evil. Amen.

'Whence' she cried, at that fair meeting,
'Comes to me this great reward?
For when first I heard the greeting
Of the Mother of my Lord,
In my womb, the joy repeating,
Leapt my babe in sweet accord!'
Festum Matris gloriosae Tr L. Housman

Hail Mary, full of grace, the Lord is with thee; blessed art thou among women, and blessed is the fruit of thy womb, Jesus. Holy Mary, Mother of God, pray for us sinners, now and at the hour of our death. Amen

Glory be to the Father, and to the Son, and to the Holy Spirit. As it was in the beginning, is now, and ever shall be, world without end. Amen.

JOSEPH TAKES MARY TO HIS OWN HOME

The Seventeenth Station towards the Nativity

When his mother Mary had been betrothed to Joseph, before they came together she was found to be with child of the Holy Spirit.

(Matthew 1: 18)

'Joseph, son of David, do not fear to take Mary your wife, for that which is conceived in her is of the Holy Spirit.'

(Matthew 1: 20b)

All this took place to fulfil what the Lord had spoken by the prophet: 'Behold, a virgin shall conceive and bear a son , and his name shall be called Emmanuel'

(Matthew 1: 22, 23)

✠ In the Name of the Father, and of the Son, and of the Holy Spirit. Amen.

 UR FATHER, WHO art in heaven, hallowed be thy name. Thy kingdom come; thy will be done on earth, as it is in heaven.

Joseph did not try to test your visiting messenger as did Zechariah, whose doubting response was hardly dissimilar from my response to your calls. Instead, Joseph's reception of your word was absolute and he did not waver. He had been troubled by Mary's pregnancy, and your message changed his mind as to the course of action he proposed to take. He listened for you and then listened to you.

When Joseph arises from his prayer, he acts immediately to take his betrothed as his wife. There is no turning back, no regret. He has been given an answer and he acts upon it and, perhaps, at this stage, he brings to mind those words of Isaiah.

Did your Apostle and Evangelist himself collect the material we now have included at the beginning of the Gospel of Matthew? Did the former dishonest tax collector whom you renamed, travel to Joseph's workshop in Nazareth to ask about your early life?

Joseph takes Mary as his wife to his home. How does she see her husband's workshop and home? Is his carpenter's bench well-known in Nazareth? If in the city, presumably it is not far from the home of Joachim and Ann, as at the time Nazareth was not a large city.

Did the workshop of your guardian look onto a narrow street lined with stone dwellings and cottage industries? Presumably the accommodation lay behind, perhaps with a courtyard and a kitchen detached from the house. Or was Joseph's workshop a little way from the main thoroughfare? But Mary saw it from the moment Joseph took her to his own home. Did she immediately imagine her Son intrigued at his guardian's skills, marvelling at the grain of olive wood and the colour and strength of timber from the terebinth tree? Were you schooled in the art of turning and joining?

Joseph without demur makes his home an environment in which you take your first steps in manhood.

Heavenly Father, help me to listen for and to your guidance.

Give us this day our daily bread. And forgive us our trespasses, as we forgive those who trespass against us. And lead us not into temptation, but deliver us from evil. Amen.

Then Joseph, being raised from slumber, did as the angel of the Lord had bidden him: and took unto him his wife.
                    Antiphon from first Vespers of St Joseph

Hail Mary, full of grace, the Lord is with thee; blessed art thou among women, and blessed is the fruit of thy womb, Jesus. Holy Mary, Mother of God, pray for us sinners, now and at the hour of our death. Amen

Glory be to the Father, and to the Son, and to the Holy Spirit. As it was in the beginning, is now, and ever shall be, world without end. Amen.

THE STAR

The Eighteenth Station towards the Nativity

… Wise Men from the East came… saying… 'we have seen his star in the East…'

(Matthew 2: 1, 2)

✠ In the Name of the Father, and of the Son, and of the Holy Spirit. Amen.

UR FATHER, WHO art in heaven, hallowed be thy name. Thy kingdom come; thy will be done on earth, as it is in heaven.

Who were these men who were guided by a star? Were they the last of the ancient Zoroastrians? Do they connect us with the Prophet Daniel, Babylon and the seers of Mesopotamia? Was it that the Wise Men had travelled in the company of merchants servicing Herod's royal court? Had they made the long journey on a whim? Of course not; they had done so after a meticulous study of a particular stellar phenomenon or conjunction. Was the bright star a comet, Jupiter, Venus? Do you reveal such things through the interpretation of the movement or position of the stars? Who can doubt that one way or another you gave these men the desire to seek out the Word made flesh. Indeed, as they had studied and marvelled at your celestial handiwork—their area of expertise—why would you not speak to them in a language they would understand and with which they were familiar?

So determined and full of faith were they, so convinced by what you had revealed through the firmament and, maybe, by material left by your chosen people after the exile in Babylon, that they were prepared, perhaps, to join a regular trading caravan in order to see for themselves. And to what end? We know little save that tantalizingly short narrative in Matthew's Gospel. However, the determination and resolution of these men to seek you out in the Bethlehem house, first calling at Herod's court for further directions, is a lesson to us in action.

It was the bright star that had alerted the astrologers and astronomers to a matter worthy of study and investigation. You were leading them so that the glory of the Word would enlighten their lives and their return home. We know that there are those good men and women through whom you can shine on others.

And I know that this is my vocation too. May I fulfil this vocation and show the determination of the Wise Men.

Give us this day our daily bread. And forgive us our trespasses, as we forgive those who trespass against us. And lead us not into temptation, but deliver us from evil. Amen.

To the Child of God today
Wise Men rightful homage pay.
Whom, immeasurably great,
Chaldean sages venerate,
To whose coming, man to save,
All the prophets witness gave.
From the Sarum sequence for The Epiphany

Hail Mary, full of grace, the Lord is with thee; blessed art thou among women, and blessed is the fruit of thy womb, Jesus. Holy Mary, Mother of God, pray for us sinners, now and at the hour of our death. Amen

Glory be to the Father, and to the Son, and to the Holy Spirit. As it was in the beginning, is now, and ever shall be, world without end. Amen.

BETHLEHEM: AND JOSEPH RESPONDS TO THE CENSUS

The Nineteenth Station towards the Nativity

But you, O Bethlehem Ephrathah, who are little to be among the clans of Judah…

Micah 5: 2a

✠ In the Name of the Father, and of the Son, and of the Holy Spirit. Amen.

 UR FATHER, WHO art in heaven, hallowed be thy name. Thy kingdom come; thy will be done on earth, as it is in heaven.

And so your prophet Micah, preaching in the grim circumstances of the collapse of the northern kingdom of Israel and the unenviable situation in the southern kingdom of Judah, sees in the midst of the destruction and corruption a glimmer of hope; hope that you gave him, his contemporaries and succeeding generations. These were the words that the scribes could recite before King Herod and in the presence of the Wise Men. You would bless this little town with the birth of our Saviour, with the birth of the Word made flesh, the Bread of life.

This was not an insignificant place as it was David's first city and David's birthplace. (David's second city was the city he made the nation's capital — Jerusalem, where you would taste your passion and death.) Bethlehem Ephrathah — significantly, the House of Bread, the place of Truthfulness — was, therefore, of the utmost importance, small though it was. Towards it Joseph and Mary would travel in some difficulty we might imagine. But they were compelled to make the journey at the insistence of the Roman authorities. It is perhaps odd that Rome would be concerned over the tribe or traditional homeland of those who were now their citizens. However, Rome controlled Palestine through their puppet-king, Herod the Great, who was always anxious to convince the people of his suitability and worthiness to sit upon the throne of David. So Joseph, of the House of David and, therefore, of the tribe of Judah (and from other sources in the early Church, we know that Mary was of the same house and tribe) travelled to Bethlehem on foot or, if fortunate, by mule or donkey with his heavily-pregnant wife.

If I have to suffer hardship during the course of my vocation, let me not waver.

Give us this day our daily bread. And forgive us our trespasses, as we forgive those who trespass against us. And lead us not into temptation, but deliver us from evil. Amen.

O Root of Jesse, which standest for an ensign of the people, at whom kings shall shut their mouths, to whom the Gentiles shall seek: Come and deliver us, and tarry not.
The third Great 'O' Antiphon

Hail Mary, full of grace, the Lord is with thee; blessed art thou among women, and blessed is the fruit of thy womb, Jesus. Holy Mary, Mother of God, pray for us sinners, now and at the hour of our death. Amen

Glory be to the Father, and to the Son, and to the Holy Spirit. As it was in the beginning, is now, and ever shall be, world without end. Amen.

The Inn, the House and the Manger

The Twentieth Station towards the Nativity

And Joseph also went… to the city of David, which is called Bethlehem, because he was of the house and lineage of David.
Luke 2: 4

✠ In the Name of the Father, and of the Son, and of the Holy Spirit. Amen.

 ur FATHER, WHO art in heaven, hallowed be thy name. Thy kingdom come; thy will be done on earth, as it is in heaven.

Heavenly Father, there they were at last, their journey complete, a few miles south of Jerusalem, exhausted and anxious to find some rest for the night. And yet, both Mary and Joseph had already put their absolute trust in you. Were they not confident that you would provide shelter? It cannot be doubted. Was Joseph's connection with Bethlehem merely historic in that he had no intimate family there, no close relations? Perhaps later, was he able to seek out a remote cousin or two with whom the Holy Family could stay once the child was born?

Their journey had begun some days ago in Nazareth. Perhaps they had been able to rest along the way and in Jerusalem. Indeed, was Joseph known there as an itinerant carpenter who had worked on Herod the Great's rebuilding of the temple? However, now that they were in Bethlehem, there was a pressing need for accommodation, for a place to give birth. The donkey ride over rough terrain made a protracted labour less likely. Help me to immerse myself in this narrative in order to understand more fully the generosity of the Holy Incarnation, and the dedication of Mary and Joseph.

Was this small city then seething with an increased population, and were there more Roman officials than usual? Was this a census station for a much larger area than the limits of Bethlehem?

And was the inn Joseph found situated on the edge of the city? Perhaps it nestled at the foot of the hill where the lambs for the temple were bred and raised? Even the inn was full, and here we imagine a rather random group of small dwellings of plastered brick contained within a walled courtyard, where travellers could stay. The owner's house would have been larger—rectangular, perhaps, with a few animals stalled on the ground floor and living quarters for the household on a mezza-nine accessible by a wooden ladder, not an easy approach for Mary. Was it in such a situation that the Holy Family was generously invited to take rest? But there was no place for a new-born baby and, in antici-pating the need for a cot, did Joseph ask for something suitable? Was he permitted to help himself to whatever he thought suitable from the stable below? And did he find there a manger in the corner, no longer in use? Did he then carry it up the ladder, filled with fresh hay having made sure that it was in reasonable order? Did he study its construction with a critical carpenter's eye and then praise you for finding them a man and his wife happy to fulfil their duty in extending a helpful hand to strangers in the land?

O Heavenly Father, assist me to place myself within sight of this scene in order to begin to understand humility.

Give us this day our daily bread. And forgive us our trespasses, as we forgive those who trespass against us. And lead us not into temptation, but deliver us from evil. Amen.

O Dayspring, Brightness of light everlasting, and Sun of Righteousness: Come and enlighten him that sitteth in darkness and the shadow of death.
                                    The fifth Great 'O' Antiphon

Hail Mary, full of grace, the Lord is with thee; blessed art thou among women, and blessed is the fruit of thy womb, Jesus. Holy Mary, Mother of God, pray for us sinners, now and at the hour of our death. Amen

Glory be to the Father, and to the Son, and to the Holy Spirit. As it was in the beginning, is now, and ever shall be, world without end. Amen.

The Wise Men begin their Journey

The Twenty-first Station towards the Nativity

A multitude of camels shall cover you, the young camels of Midian and Ephah; all those from Sheba shall come. They shall bring gold and frankincense and proclaim the praise of the Lord.

Isaiah 60: 6

… in the days of Herod the king, behold, Wise Men from the East came to Jerusalem, saying, 'Where is he who has been born king of the Jews? For we have seen his star in the East, and have come to worship him.'

Matthew 2: 1, 2

'… O Bethlehem… from you shall come forth for me one who is to be ruler in Israel, one whose origin is from old, from ancient days.'

Micah 5: 2

...and going into the house they saw the child with Mary his mother, and they fell down and worshipped him. Then...they offered him...gold, frankincense and myrrh.'

Matthew 2: 11

✠ In the Name of the Father, and of the Son, and of the Holy Spirit. Amen.

 UR FATHER, WHO art in heaven, hallowed be thy name. Thy kingdom come; thy will be done on earth, as it is in heaven.

For how many weeks did this caravan, a caravan of camels, maybe, travel from Mesopotamia to Jerusalem? Let us suppose it to carry merchants with whom the doughty astrologers had joined for the journey. What was their route? Presumably, they took the safest trading route. Did they travel several hundred miles and follow the route Zerubbabel took in 538 BC when returning from exile in Babylon to Jerusalem—along the south side of the Euphrates to Aleppo, and then due south? Were the Wise Men to follow five hundred years later by the same route in order to seek you? Here there is exquisite symmetry and, perhaps, irony.

Your prophet, Isaiah III, looking forward to the restoration following the return from exile in Babylon, foresaw a time when Jerusalem would once again attract wealth and grandeur and lavish trading and caravans of camels. And here, hundreds of years later, with merchants trading at Herod's court, we have the Wise Men anxiously making enquiries of the duty officials as to where your birthplace might be. The chronology we do not know but we suspect that this might have occurred a little time after your Holy Nativity, when you were better established in your infancy and perhaps housed more securely in Bethlehem.

The scribes, almost nonchalantly it seems, produced the information about Bethlehem to the enquiring Wise Men. Perhaps they had often read Micah's passage without any deep thought or consideration. Herod, however, with a charming smile towards the visitors, planned his murderous onslaught on the Holy Innocents of Bethlehem. The Wise Men gratefully accepted the directions they had been given and, perhaps leaving the merchants camping in Jerusalem, travelled south. At what stage might they have purchased from those merchants a golden casket of frankincense and myrrh to leave at your feet?

They left their gifts and returned home another way carrying in their hearts something more precious, their lives now illumined by your radiance, a radiance that would lighten the Gentiles, far brighter even than the star they had followed so assiduously. Let me contemplate: gold for a king; incense for God; myrrh for a mortal.

Give us this day our daily bread. And forgive us our trespasses, as we forgive those who trespass against us. And lead us not into temptation, but deliver us from evil. Amen.

The Sages beholding the star, said one to another: This is the sign of a mighty King: forth fare we, and let us seek him: and let us offer him gifts; gold, incense and myrrh.
            Antiphon for first Vespers of Epiphany

Hail Mary, full of grace, the Lord is with thee; blessed art thou among women, and blessed is the fruit of thy womb, Jesus. Holy Mary, Mother of God, pray for us sinners, now and at the hour of our death. Amen

Glory be to the Father, and to the Son, and to the Holy Spirit. As it was in the beginning, is now, and ever shall be, world without end. Amen.

THE BETHLEHEM HILLSIDE

The Twenty-second Station towards the Nativity

And in that region there were shepherds out in the field, keeping watch over their flock by night.

Luke 2: 8

Get you up to a high mountain, O Zion, herald of good tidings, lift up your voice with strength, O Jerusalem, herald of good tidings, lift it up, fear not; say to the cities of Judah, 'Behold your God!' He will feed his flock like a shepherd, he will gather the lambs in his arms, he will carry them in his bosom, and gently lead those that are with young.

Isaiah 40: 9, 11

✠ In the Name of the Father, and of the Son, and of the Holy Spirit. Amen.

 ur FATHER, who art in heaven, hallowed be thy name. Thy kingdom come; thy will be done on earth, as it is in heaven.

The Wise Men came from the lands of the Gentiles, much removed from those of your chosen people, anxious to seek out the truths of their research: the local shepherds were not in the least learned and considered inferior men as their duties did not always permit them to perform their religious observances in the ways dictated by the scribes and Pharisees. We must assume that your evangelist, Luke, was meticulous in collecting this background to your birth in Bethlehem; he was concerned that we appreciate the significance of the narrative. Why were these men particularly sensitive to your call to worship? Rough and gruff and hardened to the extremes of the weather they might have been, but you encouraged them away from the hillside, nevertheless, to see a baby. Leaving the flocks that grazed there on the green grass of the area, they scrambled down the hillside to the inn at its foot. Doubtless they left the sheep in the charge of younger members of their fraternity. After all, they were responsible for providing good quality lambs for the Temple sacrifices in Jerusalem, only a few miles away. Here within an enclosure at the foot of the hill were probably many stone dwellings used mostly for travellers, the largest housing the owner and his wife. As no pregnant stranger in this land would ever be left to her own devices, were Mary and Joseph accommodated there?

The shepherds were local men who lived apart from the rest of the community, living their lives almost leper-like. You called them down the hill to be the first to seek you and find you. Is it surprising to us that you should first invite the least of the community? No, for we know that you yourself are the good shepherd who feeds the whole of his flock with his own body and blood.

Luke pictures your call to those shepherds with brilliant, luminous and voluminous brush strokes of the painter he is reputed to have been, emphasizing the strength of your call to them.

May we too never ignore the least of the kingdom.

Give us this day our daily bread. And forgive us our trespasses, as we forgive those who trespass against us. And lead us not into temptation, but deliver us from evil. Amen.

O Emmanuel, our King and Lawgiver, the Desire of all nations, and their salvation: Come and save us, O Lord our God.

The seventh Great 'O' Antiphon

Hail Mary, full of grace, the Lord is with thee; blessed art thou among women, and blessed is the fruit of thy womb, Jesus. Holy Mary, Mother of God, pray for us sinners, now and at the hour of our death. Amen.

Glory be to the Father, and to the Son, and to the Holy Spirit. As it was in the beginning, is now, and ever shall be, world without end. Amen.

GOD TURNS THE WORLD UPSIDE DOWN: JOSEPH IS OVERWHELMED AS THE WORLD SEEMS TO STAND STILL

The Twenty-third Station towards the Nativity

The wolf shall dwell with the lamb, and the leopard shall lie down with the kid, and the calf and the lion and the fatling together, and a little child shall lead them. The cow and the bear shall feed; their young shall lie down together; and the lion shall eat straw like the ox.

Isaiah 11: 6, 7

'But as I was going' said Joseph, 'I looked up into the air, and I saw the clouds astonished, and the fowls of the air stopping in the midst of their flight. And I looked down towards the earth, and saw a table spread, and working people sitting around it, but their hands were upon the table, and they did not move to eat. They who had meat in their

*mouths did not eat. They who lifted their hands up to their
heads did not draw them back: and they who lifted them up
to their mouths did not put anything in…'*
                              Protevangelium XIII: 2–6

✠ In the Name of the Father, and of the Son, and of the
Holy Spirit. Amen.

 UR FATHER, WHO art in heaven, hallowed be thy
name. Thy kingdom come; thy will be done on
earth, as it is in heaven.

You gave your prophet Isaiah some strange words to
utter many centuries ago. He declared that in due time
the Davidic root would spring to life and true peace
would result. We know this to be true for we now
know that your Peace is your kingdom and you the
kingdom of Heaven itself. But what of this Utopian
world? Does Isaiah truly see a land before the Fall of
Adam and Eve; does he imagine the world of Eden?
Does he envisage perfection in terms of the reversal of
everything he has experienced? Do you not inspire him
to conclude, quite simply, that nothing is beyond your
power; that even though nature is your medium, your
actions may be contrary to what is known of nature or
expected? Is Isaiah not telling us that the Messiah may
be to many as someone of unbelievable or impossible
perfection? He illustrates this wonder at you by
reminding his hearers and readers that you are
omnipotent and can turn the world upside down and
inside out, or cause it to stand still should you deem

it necessary; that in your Messiah you will give us something as unexpected and as surprising as the scene he pictures wherein the carnivore and herbivore enjoy each other's company and thrive on the plants of the field. (And yet, paradoxically, these extraordinary things do happen among the young animals from time to time, and a little child can often achieve that which an adult cannot.)

This theme of your absolute control over your handiwork is further illustrated some eight hundred years later in one of the non-canonical writings — *The Evangelium* — and shows your dutiful guardian, Joseph, in search of a midwife and finding the prospect of Mary's giving birth to his Saviour suddenly overwhelming and impossible to comprehend. And for a moment or two he sees the world, along with its mundane and ordinary business, stall and allow him time to grasp something of your grandeur and power.

That you entered humanity through Mary for us, is a truth of utmost beauty.

Give us this day our daily bread. And forgive us our trespasses, as we forgive those who trespass against us. And lead us not into temptation, but deliver us from evil. Amen.

Heirs are we of a great mystery: the womb of her that knew not man is become the temple of the Godhead: he, of a Virgin incarnate, suffereth no defilement: all nations shall gather, saying: Glory to thee, O Lord.

Antiphon, second Vespers of the Circumcision

Hail Mary, full of grace, the Lord is with thee; blessed art thou among women, and blessed is the fruit of thy womb, Jesus. Holy Mary, Mother of God, pray for us sinners, now and at the hour of our death. Amen.

Glory be to the Father, and to the Son, and to the Holy Spirit. As it was in the beginning, is now, and ever shall be, world without end. Amen.

The Nativity and the Adoration of the Shepherds

The Twenty-fourth Station towards the Nativity

'For to you is born this day in the city of David a Saviour, who is Christ the Lord. And this shall be a sign for you: you will find a baby wrapped in swaddling cloths and lying in a manger.' When the angels went away from them into heaven, the shepherds said to one another, 'Let us go over to Bethlehem and see this thing, which the Lord has made known to us. And they went with haste, and found Mary and Joseph, and the baby lying in a manger. And when they saw it they made known the saying which had been told them concerning the child.

Luke 2: 11, 12, 15–17

❊

✠ In the Name of the Father, and of the Son, and of the Holy Spirit. Amen.

 UR FATHER, WHO art in heaven, hallowed be thy name. Thy kingdom come; thy will be done on earth, as it is in heaven.

We try to picture the scene on the mezzanine of that house in Bethlehem. Does Joseph respectfully descend the wooden ladder to be among the animals below? Does he find an old pole-lathe and set about repairing it beside the beasts in the stalls while Mary, attended by the owner's wife, brings to birth your Holy Word into the world? Is Joseph content to remain there until summoned by your first cry, his role of guardian begun? Does he first walk backwards to the wall to obtain a view of the upper level? Does he then see his wife reclining on a mattress with the new-born child freshly swaddled and in the manger he provided earlier? Is he momentarily overcome with emotion and does he wipe away a tear just as the large wooden door bursts open and a number of rough-looking workmen tumble in noisily but open-mouthed with delight? The upper level is low enough for those on the earthen floor to view the entire scene above. Do the shepherds in admiration and awe and moved by an inexplicable feeling of devotion fall to their knees one by one as Mary smiles at them? Does the midwife give them a patient but not unfriendly scowl and Joseph extend a hand to them?

This comfortable and lovely scene is much in everyone's mind. We are moved by it especially, knowing that, in thirty years or so, this child will be the price to be paid for the Redemption of mankind, of my

Redemption. Let us give thanks in the knowledge that you are as present in your most Holy Sacrament of the Altar as you were in that manger in Bethlehem.

Allow me to kneel there before your Holy Family.

Give us this day our daily bread. And forgive us our trespasses, as we forgive those who trespass against us. And lead us not into temptation, but deliver us from evil. Amen.

Today the Christ is born: today hath a Saviour appeared: today on earth Angels are singing, Archangels rejoicing: today the righteous exult and say, Glory to God in the highest. Alleluia!

Antiphon, second Vespers Christmas Day

Ye shepherds tell us, whom saw ye? And proclaim the nativity of Christ. We beheld the child, wrapped in swaddling clothes, and the Angel choirs, giving praise to the Saviour.

Antiphon in the Octave of the Circumcision

Hail Mary, full of grace, the Lord is with thee; blessed art thou among women, and blessed is the fruit of thy womb, Jesus. Holy Mary, Mother of God, pray for us sinners, now and at the hour of our death. Amen.

Glory be to the Father, and to the Son, and to the Holy Spirit. As it was in the beginning, is now, and ever shall be, world without end. Amen.

Lightning Source UK Ltd.
Milton Keynes UK
UKOW04f1103170915

258795UK00001B/3/P